D0765714

FREDDIE THE FROG® AND THE THUMP IN THE NIGHT

by **Sharon Burch**

illustrated by
Tiffany Harris

Adapted into storybook text by
Deborah Watley

· 1ST ADVENTURE: TREBLE CLEF ISLAND ·

MYSTIC PUBLISHING, INC. • Mystic, Iowa

To Bill, my husband and best friend, who inspires me to go further, and encourages me to try; without you, this book would not be. To Alex and Morgan, you are truly blessings from above.
—S.B.

To Travis, Ben, Daniel, and Annika—all my love.
—T.H.

Text © 2003 by Sharon Burch
Illustrations © 2003 by Tiffany Harris

Printed in China by Jade Productions, April 2015.

Book design and production by *The Kids at Our House.*
The artwork in *Freddie the Frog® and The Thump in the Night* was rendered in watercolor and ink on drawing paper.

The sound track on the audio CD accompanying *Freddie the Frog® and The Thump in the Night* was composed and performed by Grant Wood with the exception of public domain musical quotations and songs of *Twinkle, Twinkle* and *Little Star. The Hokey Pokey* written by Roland Lawrence Laprise used by permission of Sony/ATV Tunes LLC.

Narration by Jonathan White.

Publisher's Cataloging-in-Publication Data
Provided by Quality Books Inc.

Burch, Sharon (Sharon Kay)
     Freddie the frog and the thump in the night/written by Sharon Burch; illustrated by Tiffany Harris:
   adapted into storybook text by Deborah Watley. —1st ed.
     p. cm. -(1st adventure. Treble Clef Island)
   SUMMARY: Freddie the frog introduces readers to the treble clef, which serves as a map of where he lives.
     Audience: Ages 4-9
     LCCN 2004101582
     ISBN 13: 978-09747454-9-7   ISBN 0-9747454-9-9

I. Frogs—juvenile fiction.   2. Music—juvenile fiction.   [1. Frogs—Fiction. 2. Music—fiction.]
I. Harris, Tiffany.   II. Watley, Deborah.   III. Title.   IV. Title: Thump in the night

PZ7.B91586Thu2004   [E]
                    QBI04-200055

10 9 8 7 6 5 4

This is Freddie. Freddie loved to sing. Not the usual croaking noises that frogs make, but songs like "Twinkle, Twinkle, Little Star" and "Froggy Went A'Courting." Music was very alive where Freddie lived, because...

...Freddie lived on the far north side of Treble Clef Island. This map of Treble Clef Island is called a staff. Freddie and his parents lived where the top line is.

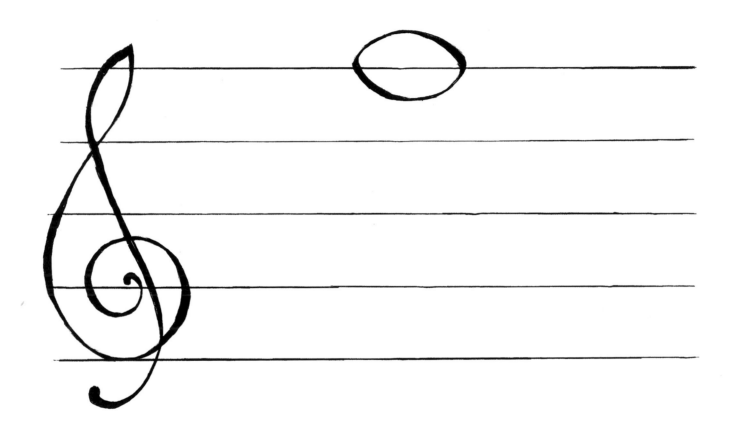

They lived in a deep, tall forest filled with ferns and fireflies. Usually the forest was a great place for a frog to live, but one very hot summer no rain fell. All the tasty bugs buzzed away to find cooler places.

Freddie's parents knew they had to find bugs or the family would starve. It was too dangerous for Freddie to travel with them, so he had to stay at home. This was the first time they had left Freddie alone overnight. With farewell hugs and kisses, Freddie's mom and dad started on their journey to find food—without their son.

At first, Freddie felt scared and lonely. "What if a burglar broke into my house?" he thought.

"Or what if I can't figure out how to toast my toadster waffle?"
"Or, what if…"

"Wait, I can do whatever I want! No one will tell me to take out the trash or turn down my music." Freddie grinned. "This could be great!"

He hopped over to the stereo and pumped up the music so loud the leaves on his tree house started to shake wildly. "BUM, bum, bum, ba, BUM, bum, bum, ba, BUM....Yeah!" Freddie finally tuckered out. He flopped into bed and did not bother to take a bath or brush his gums.

Suddenly, in the middle of the night, a loud thumping noise jolted Freddie out of his sleep. **THUMP....THUMP....THUMP....THUMP.**

"Oh, no! Someone's coming to get me!" Freddie's heart thumped now! Terrified, Freddie huddled under his blanket. "Please go away, please go away," he whimpered.

But it didn't.

THUMP....THUMP....THUMP....THUMP.

All night it thumped.

As dawn peeked through the windows, Freddie could not stand it anymore.

THUMP....THUMP....THUMP....THUMP.

He felt a bit curious. He felt a little brave. Slowly, Freddie crept to the front door. The sound grew even louder when he opened the door.

THUMP....THUMP....THUMP....THUMP.

"What is it?" Freddie wondered. The sound echoed from across the river.

The Crocodile River flowed through the middle of Treble Clef Island, and frog-eating crocodiles swam in it and basked on the sandy banks.

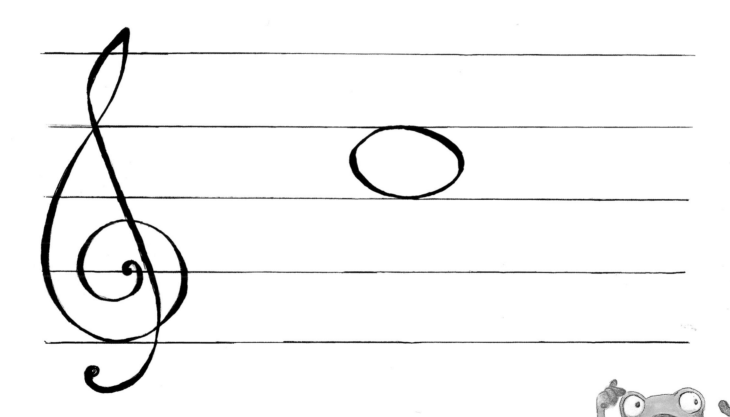

"Yikes! How can I get across without becoming breakfast?"

He began to climb down the tree. Freddie paused and peered across the river. He had heard stories about humongous gray monsters that lived beyond Crocodile River.

In the distance, he saw a gray lump
moving back and forth. Freddie had heard the gray
monsters could squish frogs in a single step!
Just then, he saw what he had been looking for…a bridge! Made from
huge logs and ropes, it swayed and creaked in the breeze.
Freddie scurried down the tree. He gulped.
"I must be brave," he thought. The little green frog hopped to the bridge.

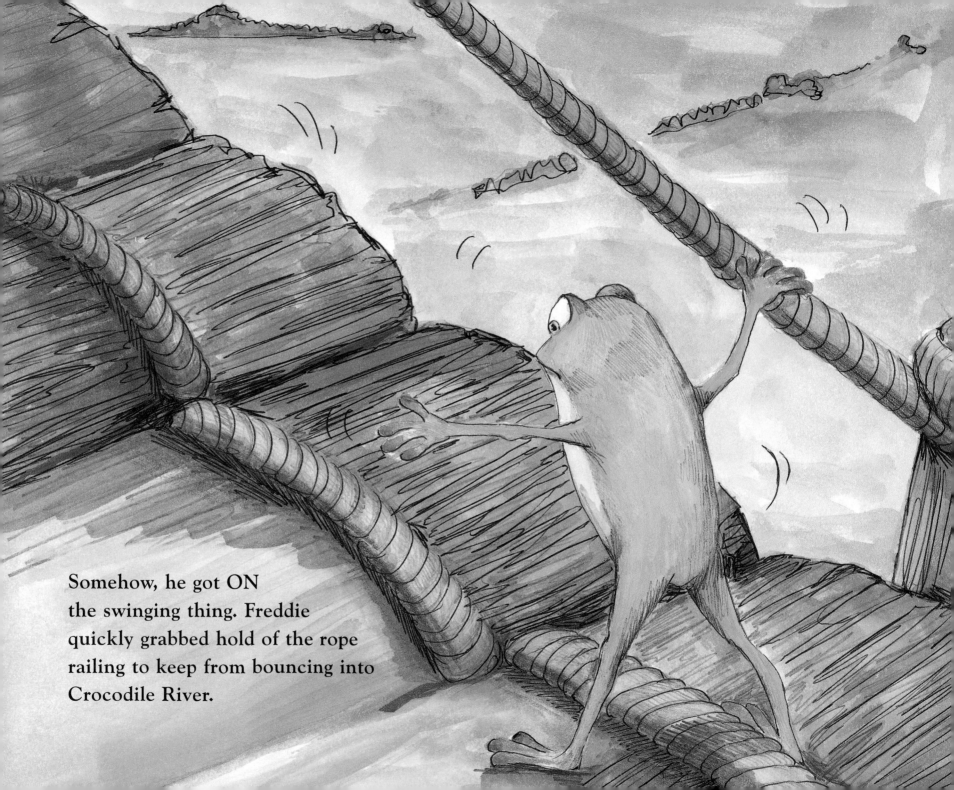

Somehow, he got ON the swinging thing. Freddie quickly grabbed hold of the rope railing to keep from bouncing into Crocodile River.

Between the logs, he could see the water swirling far below him.

THUMP....THUMP....THUMP....THUMP.

The bridge shook violently with every thump. "Hang on, Freddie!" he told himself.

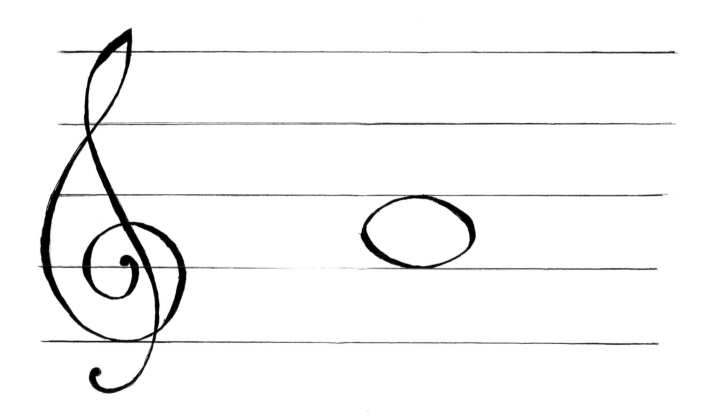

Freddie knew he should not look down anymore. He fixed his eyes on the other side of the river, where acres of **A**zaleas covered the ground. As far as he could see, the pink flowers grew beside the river like a soft, rippling ribbon.

THUMP!

As he struggled to the end of the moving
bridge, the thumping grew even louder. Each terrible
thump bounced Freddie off his feet. Then he saw IT—an enormous
monster was walking away from him on huge thumping feet!
It made the earth shake.

The monster turned around....It saw
Freddie....It charged at Freddie!

THUMP, THUMP,
   THUMP, THUMP,
      THUMP, THUMP,
         THUMP, THUMP!

Freddie lost his footing.
Dangling from the rope,
Freddie froze in fear.

The monster swung its long nose, swished it in the air, captured Freddie, and lifted him level with its beady black eyes.

"AAAAAAAAAAAH!" screamed Freddie.

"Hey, there," said the monster, "Are you okay?"

"Don't eat me, please!" Freddie pleaded. ("Phew!" Freddie thought, "His breath smells like peanuts!")

"Why would I want to eat you? I don't eat anything that can talk," the monster said. "I eat leaves and grass and peanut butter."

"Y-y-you do?" Freddie asked. "Whew! I heard that you gray monsters squish frogs, and I thought you'd squish me and eat me."

"Nah, I'm an elephant. My name is Eli."

"I-I-I'm Freddie. A-a-are you sure you're not a monster?" Freddie stammered and then asked indignantly, "Hey! Why are you making so much noise?"

"My mom and dad had to leave to search for food and I felt all alone. I couldn't sleep, so I just kept walking back and forth," Eli confessed.

"Wow! My parents are searching for food, too!" exclaimed Freddie. Then, with a sheepish grin, Freddie admitted, "Your thumping scared me to death!"

"Sorry," Eli said. Suddenly, his eyes lit up and he asked, "Hey, do you want to stay and play with me?"

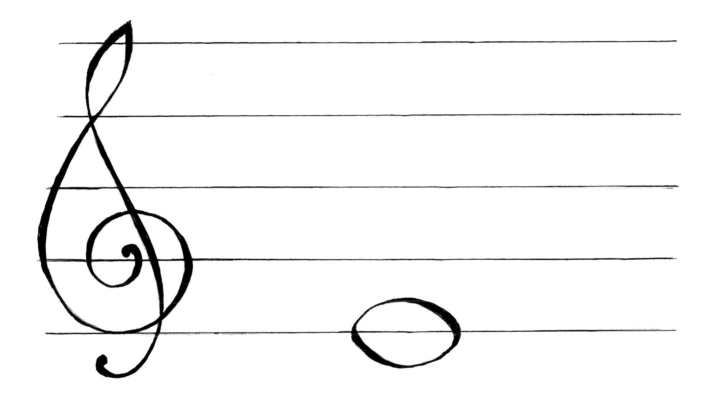

Freddie stayed at **E**li's home all day. They played hide-and-seek in the azaleas and checkers in Eli's room.

Freddie taught Eli his favorite songs, and Eli taught Freddie how to do the "Hokey Pokey."

That evening, Freddie hopped happily back to his home. Just as he reached his tree, his parents returned with their bags full of yummy bugs. At dinner, he told them all about his new friend Eli, the elephant, who was not a monster, even if he was humongous.

The next morning Freddie and his parents hopped across the bridge to meet Eli. Eli's parents had successfully returned with food. The elephants invited the frogs to a picnic under the elm trees near their home. They feasted and shared stories. The two families quickly became the best of friends.

One day, Freddie was riding on top of Eli's head, gazing down at the azaleas.

"What are you thinking about, Freddie?" Eli asked.

"I get awfully lonely when my mom and dad go away to find bugs," Freddie said. "I'm glad I can play with you during the day. I don't like being by myself."

Eli thought for a while. "What if we could stay together the whole time our parents have to be away?"

"That would be great!" replied Freddie. "But, you are too big to sleep in my room." Freddie slumped back down. The two friends stood in the flowers thinking.

"I have an idea!" Freddie exclaimed. "We could build you a hut right next to our tree house! You can stay with me when your parents have to leave."

"Great thinking!" replied Eli. "And you can sleep at my place when your parents search for bugs!"

"What if you roll over in your sleep and squish me?" Freddie asked worriedly.

"Oh, that wouldn't be good," Eli said. They both thought some more.

Then Eli smiled, "I know! We could build a tree house right next to my hut!"
"Perfect!" grinned Freddie. "Let's go ask our parents."

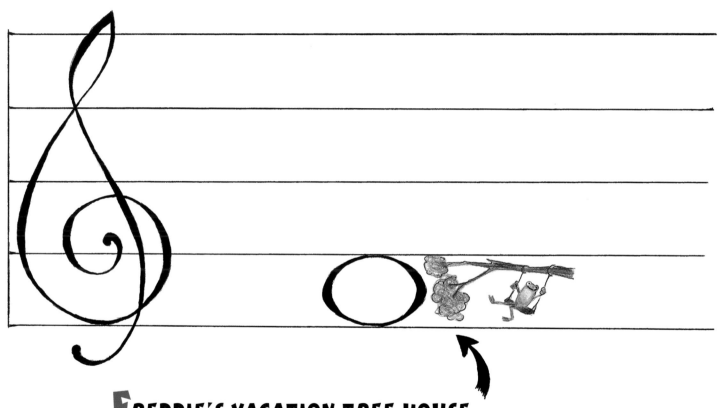

FREDDIE'S VACATION TREE HOUSE

For the rest of that hot summer and into the fall, Freddie and Eli's parents took turns going on trips, and the boys played together and stayed together.

All too soon, winter came to the island, blowing chilly breezes. Freddie's gums chattered too much for him to sing.

"It's time for us to hibernate, Freddie," said his mom. Freddie didn't want to, but he just could not stop shivering.

So, with a sad heart, Freddie helped his parents dig down deep in the mud of the riverbank. They covered themselves in mud blankets and slept warm and toasty all winter. Freddie dreamed of playing with Eli and all the fun things they would do when spring came.

When the azaleas began to bloom in the spring, Eli knew it was time. Each day he anxiously waited on the opposite riverbank for Freddie to wake up and crawl out of the mud. One warm afternoon, Freddie opened his sleepy eyes eager to see his elephant friend. He wriggled out of the mud, stretched his legs and looked all around for Eli. After sleeping so long his froggy mind did not think straight.

He spotted Eli on the other side of the river.

"Eli!" he yelled, and without another thought, he jumped over the river! Well, almost.

Eli saw Freddie's leap and screamed,

"Freddie! NO-o-o-o-o!"

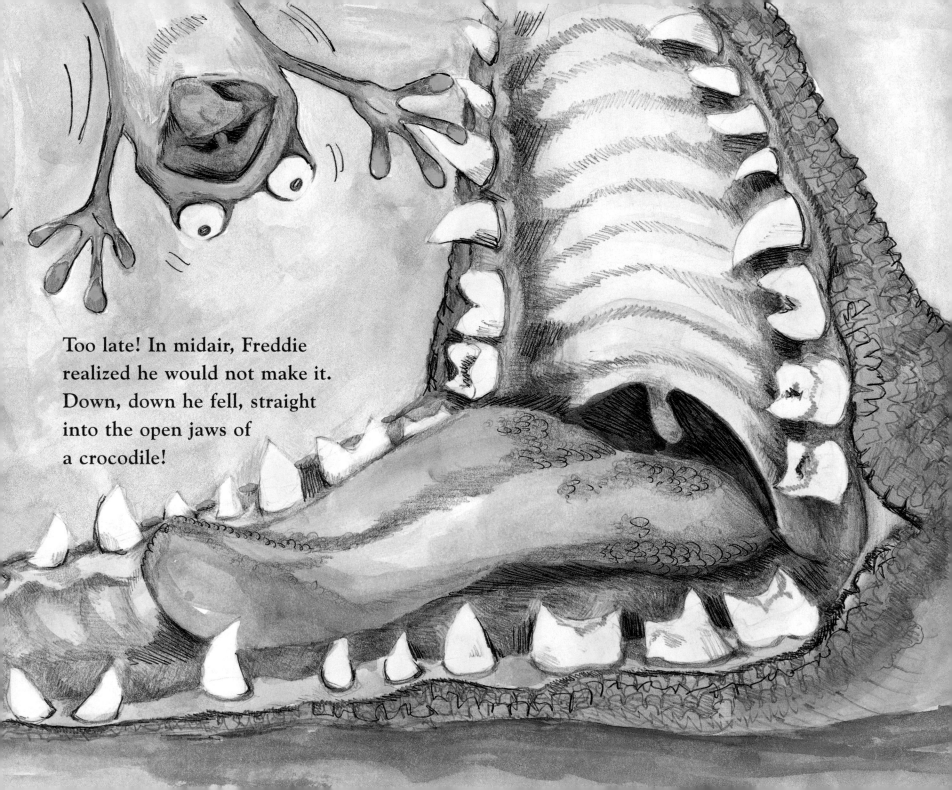

Too late! In midair, Freddie realized he would not make it. Down, down he fell, straight into the open jaws of a crocodile!

Gulp! What a surprise for the crocodile! Enjoying a big yawn in the warm, lazy afternoon, she never saw Freddie coming. But she sure felt him plop onto her tongue and slide down her throat!

Eli thumped away as fast as he could to find help. Terrified, Freddie hopped and flopped inside the belly of the crocodile.

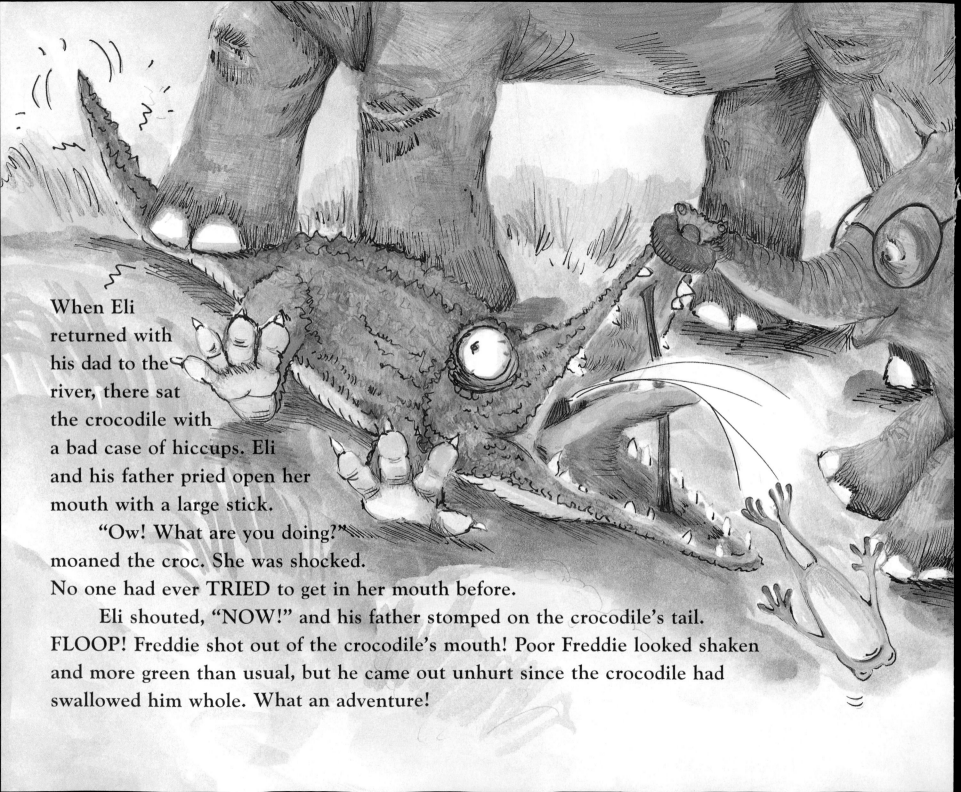

When Eli
returned with
his dad to the
river, there sat
the crocodile with
a bad case of hiccups. Eli
and his father pried open her
mouth with a large stick.

"Ow! What are you doing?"
moaned the croc. She was shocked.
No one had ever TRIED to get in her mouth before.

Eli shouted, "NOW!" and his father stomped on the crocodile's tail.
FLOOP! Freddie shot out of the crocodile's mouth! Poor Freddie looked shaken
and more green than usual, but he came out unhurt since the crocodile had
swallowed him whole. What an adventure!

Eli and Freddie shared many adventures that summer, but none as scary and dangerous as the crocodile encounter. They played lots of hide-and-seek in the azaleas. They also liked to listen to their favorite music while dancing on Eli's bed. And although their parents did not have to take trips to find bugs and peanuts that summer, Freddie and Eli still spent many nights sleeping over at their vacation homes.

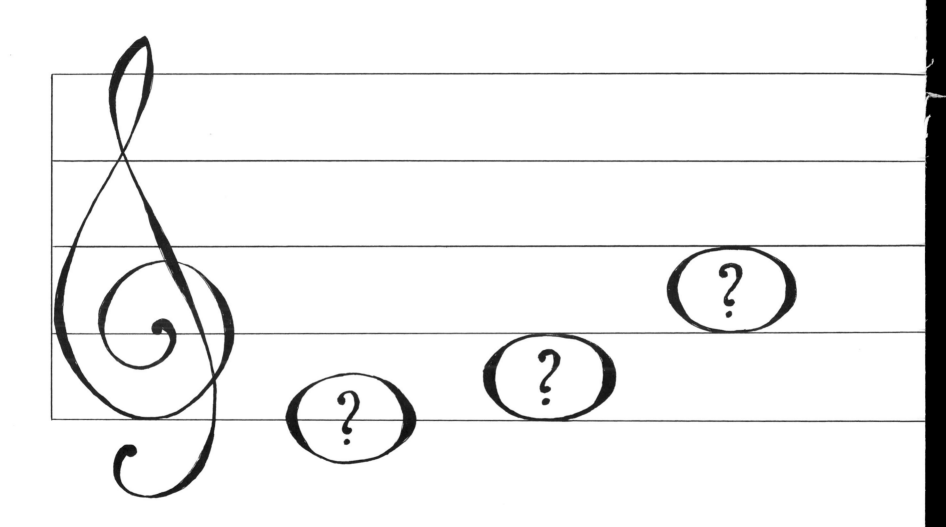

Do you remember what or who is at each place on the staff?

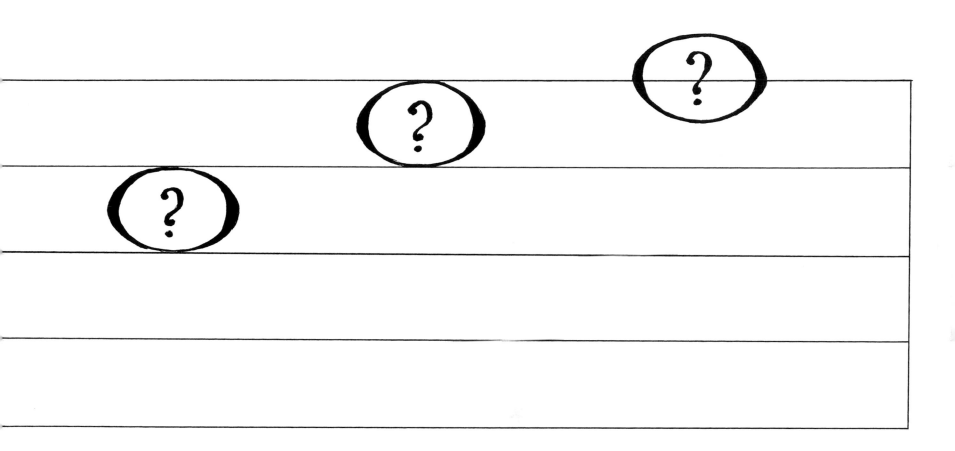

(Turn the page to find the answers.)

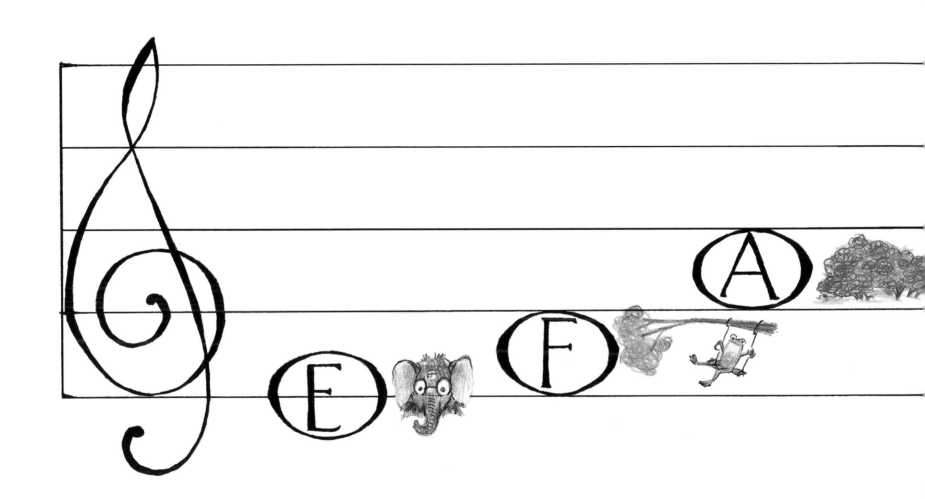

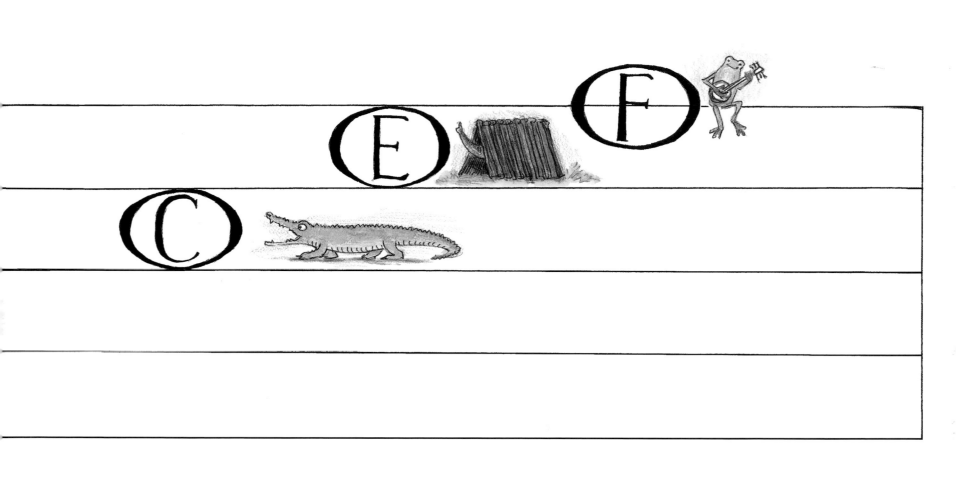

FREDDIE the FROG® BOOKS

Discover the magic of Freddie the Frog® (and learn music too!)

Freddie the Frog® and the Thump in the Night
1st Adventure: Treble Clef Island
Book/CD

Thump in the Night
Flashcard Set 1

Bass Clef Monster
Flashcard Set 2

Freddie the Frog® and the Bass Clef Monster
2nd Adventure: Bass Clef Monster
Book/CD

Crater Island
Flashcard Set 3

Freddie the Frog® and the Mysterious Wahooooo
3rd Adventure: Tempo Island
Book/CD

Mysterious Wahooooo
Magnetic Rhythm Set

Freddie the Frog® and the Secret of Crater Island
4th Adventure: Crater Island
Book/CD

SKIDDLEY

Flying Jazz Kitten Scat Words
Flashcard Set 4

Freddie the Frog® and the Flying Jazz Kitten
5th Adventure: Scat Cat Island
Book/CD

Freddie the Frog® and the Invisible Coquí
6th Adventure: Salsa Island
Book/CD

Treble Clef Island
Poster

Freddie the Frog®
Hand Puppet and Plush Toys

Bass Clef Monster
Poster

COLORING PAGES AND GAMES
www.FreddieTheFrog.com

TEACHING MUSIC WITH FREDDIE THE FROG®
www.TeachingwithFreddieTheFrog.com